For

*To my nephew, N. Jonathan Jim,
and to the sacred language
we use to communicate*

*End sheet is Navajo rug design. Title page pottery design is
Southwest U.S., 11th-13th Century.*

*Illustrations by Woody Crumbo
used by permission of his
daughter, Minisa Crumbo*

Copyright © 1994
Peter Pauper Press, Inc.
202 Mamaroneck Avenue
White Plains, NY 10601
All rights reserved
ISBN 0-88088-447-9
Printed in Hong Kong
7   6   5   4   3   2   1

Contents

Introduction

The clanship system in Navajo culture has provided me with hours of storytelling with many grandfathers. One of them used to say, *The sacred begins at the tip of your tongue. Be careful when speaking. You create the world around you with your words.* It is only right then that through these short quotations Indian people recreate their world—the past, the present, and the future.

The following quotations have a poetic string running through them. They allow you to experience life in ways that you have never experienced it before—joy, sadness, hope, despair, experiment, creation, vision.

Although the speakers represent many different tribal groups, they have a common voice. The power of this voice moves you not because it reflects what has happened to another group of people, but because you have experienced that power, positively or negatively, yourself. And if we do not heed this voice—the words of these people—we may be destined for the same annihilation.

The American Indians have always been informed by oral tradition. They understand

that knowledge is power and that stories are full of knowledge.

American Indians have been ordained by the Holy People with the power to choose. They must begin once again to exercise that power to choose—to choose to tell their own stories. Certainly, people who spoke the words of wisdom in this book chose their words carefully, because they knew that they were children of God and that what they said would inform the world.

The Italian explorer Christopher Columbus simply verified what Indians already knew when he described them as *un gente que vive en dios—a people who live in God*. As children *en dios—in God,* they must come to understand that they may yet save the world. It must begin with simple, sanctifying words from the tips of their tongues.

Helping save the world from cultural genocide for me must begin by saving myself, and the first step toward that is affirming my identity. My identity must begin with the sacred words, *en dios—indios—in God*. I am an American Indian, not a *Native American*. Therefore, I do not hesitate to subtitle this book of quotations *Wisdom of the American Indian*.

As Bea Medicine demands, we as American Indians need to do our research and express ourselves with the confidence that stems from knowledge. I hope that one day this knowledge may be passed on by American Indians themselves in American Indian languages. This is the only *politically correct* course of action to take. I know that more books in Navajo will be coming soon. That is my duty.

R. L. J.

Voices of Creativity

The first word gives origin to the second, the first and second to the third, and third to the fourth, and so on. You cannot begin with the second word and read the poem, for the poem is itself a cumulative process, a chain of being. There is a poem in me; I have been writing it for a long time, truly, as I have heard it in my heart. It matters that, having heard it, I should write it down.

N. SCOTT MOMADAY,
Kiowa

I write on the inside of trees.

GLORIA ANZALDUA

I write about pain and recovery, I suppose, more than anything. I want to move people, cause them to experience sadness and then hope. Sometimes to laugh in the midst of despair. No matter what, hope is the outcome. I borrow from my life when I write more than anything.

DIANE E. BENSON

There is such a love of stories among Navajo people that it seems each time a group of more than two gather, the dialogue eventually evolves into sharing stories and memories, laughing, and teasing. To be included in this is a distinct way of showing affection and appreciation for each other. So it is true that daily conversations strengthen us as do the old stories of our ancestors that have been told since the beginning of the Navajo time.

LUCI TAPAHONSO,
Diné (Navajo)

At night, after the day's chores were done, one could step outside and hear the music of flutes playing in different parts of the village. This was what musically inclined men did after the evening meal, especially in the summer when it was likely to be warm inside. They took their flutes and sat outside by the door on adobe benches and played.

ALFONSO ORTIZ,
San Juan Pueblo

All the songs I play, I play for the Creator to give thanks for this talent of playing the flute.

FERNANDO CELLICION,
Zuni

I like my painting to be clean. If I go out of
the line a little, I'll fix it because I don't like
sloppy painting. The painting is a reflection on
me. It should be right.

GAIL CERNO,
Acoma

I don't remember a world without language.
From the time of my earliest childhood, there
was language. Always language, and
imagination, speculation, utters of sound.
Words, beginnings of words. What would I be
without language?

SIMON J. ORTIZ,
Acoma

Theater work is a form of self-expression like
singing, dancing, painting or sculpture. In
theater you express something from inside
yourself which in turn is communicated to
other people. That's the thrill of it. . . . You
learn more and more about yourself and about
other people.

JOHN KAUFFMAN,
Nez Percé

Story telling is a continuous circle. It is the root of our traditions. Children are the essence of life.

JENNIE SEMINOLE PARKER,
Cheyenne

We are all creators. We breathe. To speak is to form breath and to make manifest sound into the world. As I write I create myself again and again. Re-Create. And breathe. And I see that I am not one voice, but many: all colors, all sounds, all fears, all loves.

JOY HARJO,
Creek

The resident priest regularly told the people that, if they did not stop dancing and praying to the sun, moon, and stars, they would all go to hell. A half century later, the people there are still singing, dancing, and praying to the sun, moon, and stars, and so far as we know, no one has gone to hell. Everyone knows there are no Indians in hell. It is not a place designed for us.

ALFONSO ORTIZ,
San Juan Pueblo

We've got to get together and not talk about it.
Dancing is my way, the Indian way, it's our
way, a part of us, and only we know it. No one
else has it and if we don't keep it up, it's going
to fade out like our land.

ISABEL KENT,
Ute

I am me. I exist. I am a Dakotah. I
write. . . . It is an act of courage. . . it is an act
that defies oppression.

ELIZABETH COOK-LYNN,
Dakotah

I fight anger and ask for calmness.
And the voice of humility.
And the ability to write-comfort.
For the children
And selfishly, for myself.

SANDY KEWANHAPTEWA-DIXON,
Hopi

It's not enough to weave beautiful rugs. You
have to think beautiful thoughts while weaving
them.

CHARLES LOLOMA,
Hopi

Voices of a People

We have come a full circle with our culture. What was old and primitive has returned with new meaning and pride. That is what I'm painting, a new feeling, a new step, a new dance to a new song; but done with that old family pride.

TED D. PALMANTEER,
Colville

When we saw the top of the mountain from Albuquerque we wondered if it was our mountain, and we felt like talking to the ground, we loved it so, and some of the old men and women cried with joy when they reached their homes.

MANUALITO,
Diné (Navajo)

I am a Shawnee. . . . I am the maker of my own fortune, and Oh! that I could make that of my Red people, and of my country, as great as the conceptions of my mind . . .

TECUMSEH,
Shawnee

We hear about all this fighting between Navajo
and Hopi. I never seen it. It is the white man
who wants that, who says that. In the old days,
maybe it was true, but now the Navajo just
wants to live in peace.

unknown Diné (Navajo)

To know the Navajo and his problems you
must get close to him by living among them.
It is hard to gain their confidence.

SAM AHKEAH,
Diné (Navajo)

We have to live by closing the circle. . . . A
Navajo miner . . . is simply confronting a
situation at hand with the available and
appropriate tools. You work in such a world in
order to improve the life of your people.
That's closing the circle—like the hunter's
prayer. We can do this—we are strong enough
to do this—because we have family in the
truest sense, an extended family. We can
always return to our family.

unknown Diné (Navajo)

Because I was born into and come out of an oral culture, I learned early that the use of words involves responsibility and respect for oneself. . . . One does not act alone in the use of words or songs; it always involves his parents, his family and distant relatives.

LUCI TAPAHONSO,
Diné (Navajo)

To think of myself outside the context of the tribe or my family or my community would be very difficult. . . . I never felt home until I came home. When I came back here, then I began to understand, this is where I belong.

WILMA MANKILLER,
Chief of the Cherokee Nation

Many Voices, One Voice

I feel sorrow for those who put
One person, one family, one tribe
One nation above another

SANDY KEWANHAPTEWA-DIXON,
Hopi

When I learned English well . . . I found
myself *objectifying* my native language, that is,
in translation. . . . Is it possible to translate
from the Acoma language to another? Yes, I've
insisted, but I'm not sure I am convinced of it
or of how complete the translation is. Since
we're all human with the same human feelings
and responses to feelings, we understand and
share hurt, love, anger, joy, sadness, elation, a
gamut of emotions. However, human cultures
are different from each other, and unique, and
we have different and unique languages; it is
not easy to translate from one language to
another though we egotistically believe and
think we can.

SIMON J. ORTIZ,
Acoma

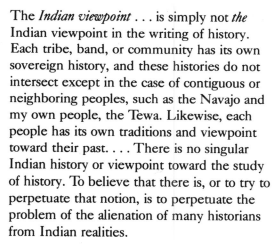

The *Indian viewpoint* . . . is simply not *the*
Indian viewpoint in the writing of history.
Each tribe, band, or community has its own
sovereign history, and these histories do not
intersect except in the case of contiguous or
neighboring peoples, such as the Navajo and
my own people, the Tewa. Likewise, each
people has its own traditions and viewpoint
toward their past. . . . There is no singular
Indian history or viewpoint toward the study
of history. To believe that there is, or to try to
perpetuate that notion, is to perpetuate the
problem of the alienation of many historians
from Indian realities.

ALFONSO ORTIZ,
San Juan Pueblo

If only one . . . speaks for us in the correct
way, that is enough to carry on our tradition.
We are still in the middle of our land . . .

LEROY OSCEOLA,
Seminole

Voices of Determination

This isn't a fun run. It has a purpose. Carry
this ear of blue corn, your mother, the entire
way. As you go, she will give you strength.
When you get back, plant from it, each of you.
Now go your way, with strength and prayer.

PRESTON KEEVAMA,
Hopi

Do you know, children, I would rather die in
the struggle for my manhood and the welfare
of my people than to remain in ignorance with
health. We cannot do any more than run the
race as far as we can. God will do the rest. Let
the heart within you throb for the betterment
of yourselves and of a nation which you claim.
You are a part of the American family:
children, to be educated for the responsibilities
that will surely come to you as a citizen of this
country.

CARLOS MONTEZUMA,
Yavapai

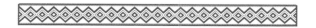

I think the whole concept of human services can be depressing because you are dealing with people and their problems. You have to learn to really substantiate your purpose in being. Let me tell you, it's frustrating, it's energy draining, it's depressing. It just takes all you have. But one of the things we have learned in our sobriety is the only way we can keep what we have, or feeling good about ourselves, is to give it away.

HAROLD BELMONT,
Suquamish/Songee

Have good heart. We're running for the people. It goes beyond athletics. . . . Turn around and shake the hand of your brother. This is more than a race. It means something.

BRUCE HAMANA,
Hopi

Long ago when the Hopi had no sheep, no horses, no burros, they had to depend for game-capturing on their legs. They then had to cultivate their legs, think much and pray much to make them swift. Men strove in earnest to rival each other in fast running, that is why the races were run . . .

unknown Hopi of the Horn Clan

To me, I can't help but get a lot of self-gratification. I've worked a long time. I can't say, *Well, I'm doing it all for Indian people.* You've got to live for yourself. You've got to feel good about what you're doing, and not just be a workhorse. I don't really like to admit it to myself, but I've worked hard to earn a title of respect. I don't feel ashamed about feeling good about it. It's a challenge.

RON SHAW,
Creek/Osage

My grandfather told me that Talking God comes around in the morning, knocks on the door, and says, *Get up, my grandchildren, it's time to run, run for health and wealth.*

REX LEE JIM,
Diné (Navajo)

My son, you know no one will help you in this world . . . You must run to that mountain and come back. That will make you strong. My son, you know no one is your friend, not even your sister, your father, or your mother. Your legs are your friends; your brain is your friend; your eye-sight is your friend; your hair is your friend; your hands are your friends; you must do something with them.

Apache father

Our grandfathers had very strong hearts, from the heat of the sweats, then plunging into the icy water, and they lived well over a hundred years.

LAME DEER

All I want is right and justice.

RED CLOUD,
Sioux

That people will continue longest in the enjoyment of peace who timely prepare to vindicate themselves and manifest a determination to protect themselves whenever they are wronged.

TECUMSEH,
Shawnee

When I am gone, think of your country. You are the chief of these people. They look to you to guide them. Always remember that your father never sold his country. . . . My son, never forget my dying words. This country holds your father's body. Never sell the bones of your father and your mother.

OLD CHIEF JOSEPH,
Nez Percé

Voices of the Land

Take the breath of the new dawn and make it part of you. It will give you strength.

unknown Hopi

What is life? It is the flash of a firefly in the night. It is the breath of a buffalo in the winter time. It is the little shadow which runs across the grass and loses itself in the Sunset.

CROWFOOT,
Blackfoot,
last words

This land is the house we have always lived in. The women, their bones are holding up the earth.

LINDA HOGAN,
Chickasaw

There was no such thing as emptiness in the world. Everywhere there was life, visible and invisible, and every object gave us a great interest to life.

unknown Lakota

How can you buy or sell the sky . . . ?

> SEALTH,
> *a Duwamish chief*

The land I stand on is my body, and I want
you to help me keep it.

> SAM JONES,
> *Miccosukee Seminole*

I find I am unbelievably various and
interesting, even to my self. I see my self a tot
beside the mystical Yukon River, she who
centered my mindset early, who colored the
lives of all my Indian forebears, that river
remote, stately, mischievous, illogical, and
rowdy, whose beauty coils unforgettable in the
seedbed of my mind.

> MARY TALLMOUNTAIN,
> *Koyukon Athabaskan*

The Indian prefers the soft sound of the wind
darting over the face of the pond, the smell of
the wind itself cleansed by a mid-day rain, or
scented with a pinon pine.

> CHIEF SEATTLE,
> *Suquamish/Duwamish*

What is man without the beasts? If all the beasts were gone, men would die from great loneliness of spirit, for whatever happens to the beasts also happens to man. All things are connected. Whatever befalls the earth befalls the sons of the earth.

CHIEF SEATTLE,
Suquamish/Duwamish

We never had a thought of exchanging our land for any other, as we think that we would not find a country that would suit us as well as this we now occupy, it being the land of our forefathers, if we should exchange our lands for any other, fearing the consequences may be similar to transplanting an old tree, which would wither and die away, and we are fearful we would come to the same. . . .

unknown Chickasaw

Shoo, that's the voice of The One Who Walks the Mountains. The Bear! Grandchild, I pray no enemy sees me as I go to my land. Though I have no relatives, though they all be captured, even so I go home because I long for my land.

ASDZAA ATSIDI,
Diné (Navajo)

If there was thick ice on top of the water I'd
get a stick or a piece of rock, break the ice,
take off my moccasins, and jump in. I'd stay in
the icy water as long as I could stand it,
turning over and over, hollering and screaming
so as to develop a good voice. Then I'd get
out and put on my moccasins and start for
home. While I'd be running on my way my
body would be covered with a thin coat of ice,
cracking all over me . . . Before going in the
hogan, I'd roll in the snow once more.

LEFT-HANDED,
Diné (Navajo)

The white man never cared for land . . .

unknown Wintu woman

If people asked me if I'd rather see the Eiffel
Tower or a rabbit, I'd pick the rabbit. Man can
learn to build an Eiffel Tower but he can't
learn what a rabbit's feelings are unless he
lives with him day in and day out. That's what
Grandpa says. The rabbit's ancestors tell him
what it was like and so he knows what we
don't know. He'll share it if we ask, but here
we are hurrying away.

DONALD WHYTE,
Ute

I didn't need a house then or a pasture. Somewhere there would be a cave, a crack in the rocks, where I could hole up during a rain. I wanted the plants and the stones to tell me their secrets. I talked to them. I roamed. I was like a part of the earth. Everything had been taken from me except myself. Now and then, in some place or other, I looked at my face in a mirror to remind myself who I was.

JOHN FIRE LAME DEER,
Sioux

I wish all to know that I do not propose to sell any part of my country, nor will I have the whites cutting our timber along the rivers, more especially the oak. I am particularly fond of the little groves of oak trees. I love to look at them, because they endure the wintry storm and the summer's heat, and—not unlike ourselves—seem to flourish by them.

TATANKA YOTANKA (SITTING BULL),
Sioux

The American Indian is of the soil, whether it be the region of forests, plains, pueblos, or mesas. He fits into the landscape, for the hand that fashioned the continent also fashioned the man for his surroundings.

CHIEF STANDING BEAR,
Oglala Sioux

As a child I understood how to give; I have forgotten this grace since I became civilized. I lived the natural life, whereas I now live the artificial. Any pretty pebble was valuable to me then; every growing tree an object of reverence. Now I worship with the white man before a painted landscape whose value is estimated in dollars! Thus the Indian is reconstructed, as the natural rocks are ground to powder and made into artificial blocks which may be built into the walls of modern society.

OHIYESA,
Sioux

The core of a tree is always the same. Look at a cross-section of a tree. From its essential center it grows, ring by ring, a ring for a year, but the core is permanent. The rings record history—of fire, drought, flood—and how the tree managed these events. But in our core, we are always Navajo, regardless of the events written in the rings or the appearance of our bark.

RODGER BOYD,
Diné (Navajo)

My father told me we should stand firm on the land. That is all we have.

MINA LANSA,
Hopi

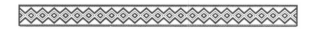

Voices of Despair

None of the plants of the past remains today.
Once from here on out you could see the land
covered with beauty, colored by many flowers
of many different plants of green, yellow, red,
and purple. But now, which of them has the
color to dress the earth in beauty? What is
there around for the animals to eat or for us to
eat? Everything around now is just plain grey.
There are no more sunflowers.

LAUGHING WOMAN,
Diné (Navajo)

What is it like for a child of any race to be
taken away from his parents and relatives at an
age when he needs their love and care the
most? What thoughts must go through a
child's mind—the fears, anxieties, the
loneliness, above all.

What are these boarding schools like? What
are their policies? I would compare these
schools to those of a military barracks, to
reformatories, to prisons.

LEROY B. SELAM,
Yakima

I hear no longer the songs of the women as they prepare the meal. . . . Only the wail of the coyote is heard. . . . We are like birds with a broken wing. My heart is cold within me. My eyes are growing dim—I am old. . . .

CHIEF PLENTY-COUPS,
Crow

The Great Spirit gave this great island to his red children. He placed the whites on the other side of the big water. They were not contented with their own, but came to take ours from us. They have driven us from the sea to the lakes—we can go no farther.

TECUMSEH,
Shawnee

It matters little where we pass the rest of our days; they are not many. A few more hours, a few more winters, and none of the children of the great tribes that once lived on this earth, or that roamed in small bands in the woods, will be left to mourn the graves of a people once as powerful and hopeful as yours.

The whites, too, shall pass—perhaps sooner than other tribes.

CHIEF SEATTLE,
Suquamish/Duwamish

Where today is the Pequot? Where are the Narragansetts, the Mohawks, the Pokanoket, and many other once powerful tribes of our people? They have vanished before the avarice and the oppression of the White Man, as snow before a summer sun.

TECUMSEH,
Shawnee

I did make up my mind in the war that I am American and I went overseas to fight for this country. Then the officers came to me while I was overseas and they told me, *You are all right. You fought for your country.* I just gave them a smile and I thought to myself, *Where is my country when I get home?*

ROBERT SPOTT,
Yurok

I can't celebrate Independence Day because I understand and see how much misery there is among our people. Indian people have lost our independence and if anything, Independence Day should be a day of mourning. As Indian nations, we are still striving to regain our independence from America.

VERNON FOSTER,
Klamath

Voices of Struggle

We lived on our land as long as we can remember. No one knows how long ago we came there. The land was owned by our tribe as far back as memory of men goes. We were living quietly on our farms. All of a sudden one white man came. We had no idea what for. This was the inspector. He came to our tribe with Rev. Mr. Hinman. These two, with the agent, James Lawrence, they made our trouble.

STANDING BEAR,
Ponca

Where the white people are, there is no peace.

TECUMSEH,
Shawnee

Hear me, my chiefs. I am tired; my heart is sick and sad. From where the sun now stands, I will fight no more forever.

CHIEF JOSEPH,
Nez Percé

I've seen him in a thousand taverns and I've seen him on a thousand juries, and in a thousand organizations and in a thousand uniforms. Every Indian has been wounded by him a thousand times before.

HANK ADAMS,
Assiniboine

This land where ye dwell I have made for you and not for others. Whence comes it that ye permit the Whites upon your lands? Can ye not live without them? . . . drive them out . . . Send them back to the lands which I have created for them and let them stay there.

CHIEF PONTIAC,
Ottawa

The whites were always trying to make the Indians give up their life and live like white men—go to farming, work hard and do as they did—and the Indians did not know how to do that, and did not want to anyway. . . . If the Indians had tried to make the whites live like them, the whites would have resisted, and it was the same way with many Indians.

WAMDITANKA (BIG EAGLE),
Santee Sioux

I hope to God you will not ask me to go to any other country except my own.

BARBONCITO,
Diné (Navajo)

Why should you take by force from us that which you can obtain by love? Why should you destroy us who have provided you with food? What can you get by war? I am not so simple as not to know that it is better to eat good meat, be well, and sleep quietly with my women and children, to laugh and be merry with the English, and being their friend, to have copper hatchets and whatever else I want.

KING POWHATAN,
Powhatan

I want to know what you are doing on this road. You scare all the buffalo away. I want to hunt in this place. I want you to turn back from here. If you don't, I will fight you again. I want you to leave . . . and turn back from here. I am your friend.

SITTING BULL,
Sioux

Americans! You have a strange cause for war
against the Navajos. We have waged war
against the New Mexicans for many years. We
have plundered their villages and killed many
of their people. You have lately commenced a
war against the same people. You are powerful.
You have great guns and many brave soldiers.
You have therefore conquered them, the very
same thing we have been attempting to do for
so many years. You now turn upon us for
attempting to do what you have done
yourselves. We cannot see why you have cause
of quarrel with us for fighting the New
Mexicans on the west, while you do the same
on the east.

ZARCILLOS LARGOS,
Diné (Navajo)

You are stronger than we. We have fought you
so long as we had rifles and powder . . . Give
us like weapons and turn us loose, we will
fight you again; but we are worn-out; we have
no more heart . . . Do with us as may seem
good to you, but do not forget we are men and
braves.

CADETTE,
Mescalero Apache

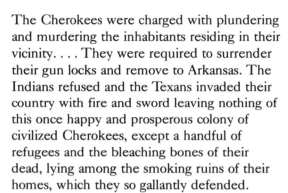

The Cherokees were charged with plundering and murdering the inhabitants residing in their vicinity. . . . They were required to surrender their gun locks and remove to Arkansas. The Indians refused and the Texans invaded their country with fire and sword leaving nothing of this once happy and prosperous colony of civilized Cherokees, except a handful of refugees and the bleaching bones of their dead, lying among the smoking ruins of their homes, which they so gallantly defended.

Texans certainly copied from the history of the Alamo and Goliad and outrivaled the Mexicans in acts of cruelty.

EMMET STARR,
Cherokee

These white people must be a great nation, [but] I fear we will suffer greatly by their coming to our country; they come for no good to us, although my father [in-law] said they were our brothers, but they do not seem to think we are like them.

CHIEF WINNEMUCCA,
Paiute

Crumbo

The Supreme Court of the United States, to this day, says that the U. S. government is free to take away Indian land, to confiscate it, extinguish aboriginal Indian title without due process of the law, without any compensation and without any regard whatever for the Fifth Amendment.

I don't see that it's proper for a government built on concepts of fairness, concepts of limited government, to find itself in a position of acting as a tyrant in its relations with the original inhabitants and governments of the continent.

ROBERT COULTER,
Pottawatomi

If anybody is crazy, it is somebody in Washington.

WOODEN LEG,
Northern Cheyenne

We can't allow Indians to do anything on their reservation that would destroy their way of life.

KEVIN GOVER,
Comanche,
describing governmental
environmental paternalism

Indian poets . . . should be writing about their brothers and sisters who have murdered their livers. We should be writing about the children born of relocation, about urban skins and res poverty, about the continual termination policies of this gov't, about 49's and snagging, about our strengths as members of specific and autonomous nations, those things we call recognized tribes.

ADRIAN C. LOUIS,
Paiute

I find that the Indian . . . stands between the visible and invisible worlds, between earth and heaven. The Indian . . . has been rejected by society and is not at home here. Neither are we at rest in the spirit world. We are neither here nor there but in the midst of the journey.

DIANE GLANCY,
Cherokee

Every year our white intruders become more greedy, exacting, oppressive, and overbearing . . . . Wants and oppressions are our lot. . . . Are we not being stripped day by day of the little that remains of our ancient liberty? . . .

TECUMSEH,
Shawnee

They seemed to overlook the fact that this is a reservation, not a concentration camp, and the only way anyone can come on the reservation and establish a business is by permission of the tribe. It's a privilege.

TOM SEGUNDO,
Tuhono O'odam

It is easy to talk about Indian unity, Indian power, the strength of the land, Indian input, but it's hard to put these ideas to work on a reservation where the main thing people want is something to eat.

LITTLE STAR,
tribe unknown

Those who hunger for monetary power and world control have used words more effectively than anyone else, including all the combined writers and artists of the world who would have it otherwise. . . . Words hypnotize, and deceive everyone at one time or another, but these hypnotic words cannot last long in the hearts of true warriors. . . . Real warriors might take different paths . . . It is the road that cannot be bought with money or evil power . . .

BARNEY BUSH,
Shawnee

I stood upon the ashes of my own home, and there I summoned the spirits of the warriors who had fallen. And as I snuffed up the smell of their blood from the ground, I swore once more eternal hatred—the hatred of an avenger!

TECUMSEH,
Shawnee

If women could go into your Congress I think justice would soon be done to the Indians.

SARAH WINNEMUCCA,
Paiute

They came out of nowhere
telling us how to eat our food
how to build our homes
how to plant crops
Need I say more of what they did?

SOGE TRACK,
Western Apache

They want all Indians trained for Merrill Lynch and doing everything that whites do, at the same time they want them down at the Santa Fe station selling pottery and painting.

VINE DELORIA, JR.,
Sioux

Voices of the Spirit

. . . I felt that somebody wanted to talk to me.
So I stood up and began to sing the first song
of my vision, the one that the two spirits had
sung to me.

> *Behold! A sacred voice is calling you!*
> *All over the sky a sacred voice is*
> *calling!*

BLACK ELK,
Sioux

We left for Denver in October of 1966. . . .
Sometimes when I'm in Denver I wish inside
that I could be back at home. . . . Living in
Denver isn't simple. I go to Christian church
when I'm in Denver. I go to make people
think that we're not superstitious about Navajo
religion. I try to worship as a Christian. If we
don't they'll probably think we're very
superstitious in the Navajo way; so we have to
try and do what we can so they won't think
we're really superstitious about everything.

ANDY BODIE,
Diné (Navajo)

I go to Bible class every week. . . . I find it contradictory to Indian belief. . . . There's sin and the devil but the Indians don't believe in those things. Then there's Christ. We say we don't need an intermediary, that we pray directly to God, and God deals directly with us. People say they need a pope or a big church to feel God but I tell them, it's all inside you. What do you need these other things for? It makes them feel better, I guess.

ANNABELLE EAGLE,
Ute

I have known both sides of living. I was mean—terrible!—before I learned blessingway.

GREYEYES STEWART,
Diné (Navajo)

People need to respect Native spirituality because it is a holistic way of life. But it is being destroyed through the desecration of our ways, the destruction of our environment and sacred sites, and the proselytizing of our people.

When you take a people's spirituality, you take away their identity and that has happened to many of our people.

OMIE BALDWIN,
Diné (Navajo)

It is a ceremony, not a performance. It is a prayer in motion. As long as the drum beats, you don't get tired.

ELENA ORTIZ,
San Juan Pueblo,
describing the Corn Dance

My heart tells me I had just as well talk to the clouds and wind, but I want to say that life is sweet, love is strong; man fights to save his life; man also kills to win his heart's desire; that is love.

CAPTAIN JACK,
Modoc

We are in danger of having our sacred spiritual ways stolen from us—the key to our survival. We must raise a united voice of protest against those who steal our spiritual traditions and tell them *You cannot have them, not today, not tomorrow, NEVER.*

DARRELL STANDING ELK,
Sicangu Lakota

Laughing Voices

It has always been a great disappointment to Indian people that the humorous side of Indian life has not been emphasized by professed experts . . . Indians have found a humorous side to nearly every problem and the experiences of life have generally been so well defined through jokes and stories that they have become a thing in themselves . . . The more desperate the problem, the more humor is directed to describe it.

VINE DELORIA, JR.,
Sioux

Us old men get to joking like that—it's sure funny to us. Some do it more than others. Some really like it. They do everything—act like Whiteman, everything. They boss you around, act like you nothing, right in front lots of people. Only we don't get mad. They just boasting, that's all. Just saying it, that's all. We been going around long time together, so we done it before.

Cibecue Apache Man

When a people can laugh at themselves and others and hold all aspects of life together without letting anybody drive them to extremes, then it seems to me that people can survive.

VINE DELORIA, JR.,
Sioux

What do I look like? The features of my face are big: a beaked nose, lips that are too sensitive, sand-brown eyes and dark eyebrows that lift one at a time like the wings of a bird, a low forehead that looks higher because of receding brown hair, an Adam's apple like a broken bone, two ears that were normal before wrestling flattened one of them. Unlike my grandfather's, my skin is not brown throughout the seasons but sallow in the winter months, though it tans dark and quickly when the sun's warmth returns. It is, as you might gather, a face I did not use to love. Today I look at it in the mirror and say, *Bruchac, you're ugly and I like you.* The face nods back at me and we laugh together.

JOSEPH BRUCHAC,
Abenaki

Voices of Wisdom

My grandchild, the whites have many things we Navajos need but cannot get. It is as though the Whites were in a grassy valley, with wagons, plows, and plenty of food, we Navajos up on a dry mesa. We can hear them talking, but we cannot get to them. My grandchild, school is the ladder. Tell our people this.

MANUELITO,
Diné (Navajo)

The council-tent is our Congress, and anybody can speak who has anything to say, women and all.

SARAH WINNEMUCCA,
Paiute

Even today we have good examples to show that without a hogan you cannot plan. You can't just go out and plan other things for your future; you have to build a hogan first. Within that, you sit down and begin to plan.

FRANK MITCHELL,
Diné (Navajo)

Protecting children from racism is every bit as important as insuring that they avoid playing with electrical sockets. Poison is poison, and ingrained oppressive cultural attitudes are at least as hard to antidote, once implanted, as are imbibed cleaning fluids. No one gains by allowing an inequitable and discriminatory status quo to persist. It's worth being a pain in the neck about.

MICHAEL A. DORRIS,
Modoc

Always remember that the greatest power that has been given to you by the Holy People is the *Power to Choose.*

WILSON ARONILTH, JR.,
Diné (Navajo)

My greatest education came from my study of my native people. I have never accepted the idea that one system has all the answers. My studies have proved me right.

It is my opinion that if anybody wants a thorough education, they should learn more than one society. This is not only an important education, it will also open their eyes to a lot of things they only fantasize about.

LINCOLN TRITT,
Neets'aii (Alaskan Native)

We serve every student that comes through this door. Remember that every student can learn. There isn't one student that cannot learn. A student may not learn through the way you teach. If so, change your approach so that that student may learn. I know I have the staff to make this an even better school.

MELVIN ARTHUR,
Principal of Rock Point
Community Secondary School,
Diné (Navajo)

When we understand our own education, then we will have self understanding: where we came from, whom we came from, who we are, what we are, why we are here and where we are going. We will then walk in beauty and everything will finish in beauty.

WILSON ARONILTH, JR.,
Diné (Navajo)

Diné education is like a horse. If you take care of your horse, and are not lazy, this horse can take care of you. . . . it will provide for you, but only if you believe in it and take care of it.

WILSON ARONILTH, JR.,
Diné (Navajo)

We never got a chance to go to school. . . .
Even though I don't know what education is
all about, I feel it is necessary, because things
aren't going backward. Now children can
better cope with what's in the future for them.
They are learning and they are retaining their
cultural heritage. I always tell my children, if
you go to school, finish and get the most out of
your education, you can have a nice job and
won't have to look around to see where your
next meal is coming from. If you have a good
education, that's your key to everything.

HELEN WOODY,
Diné (Navajo)

Western education today tends to be didactic.
Children are told—in books, lectures, film
strips, and movies—about things, but rarely do
them, experience them. Adults then test the
children by having them answer questions
about what they have *learned.*

JOSEPH BRUCHAC,
Abenaki

Sure, we want computers. We would like a PC
in every hogan. It's just we want those
computers programmed to think Navajo.

Unknown Navajo tribal official

Voices of Yesterday,
Voices of Tomorrow

I am a Neo-traditional artist/storyteller. Neo-
traditional, in that I believe in the continuous
creation theory: everything is in perpetual
renewal. Tradition and ritual are re-enactment or
reproduction, and they are accurate, hardly
variable, because they are intended to re*call*.
They are connections to the past. They are
necessary because they ground us and affirm
who we are in relation to where we have been.

ROBERT H. DAVIS,
Tlingit

Where have the elders gone? . . . Where are
they, the people who are supposed to be
leading us? . . . I'm teaching my kids that they
have to serve this tribe, that they have to give,
no matter what. We're not so much white that
we can turn our backs on the way we were
raised.

ANNABELLE EAGLE,
Ute

We are more than just our pasts. We are also reactions to the immediate present; we require rituals for contemporary themes. Form and content of older ritual are modified as they accommodate newer circumstances: the *warrior* mentality and associated rituals are now acted out on basketball courts; secret societies and their exclusivity are enacted behind closed offices in new Native corporations. Artists and writers are using the old forms, (in new variations) to address contemporary social issues. In this way, the old and the new become one thing in the present.

ROBERT H. DAVIS,
Tlingit

Who thinks about the sheep? Who thinks of making a living off the sheep? There is no one. They just want to go forward. They just get in their car, and zoom. Off they go. Who cares any more about the wisdom of the past and the way we survived on the land? I hope there may be one or two young people around who do respect that wisdom, but where are they?

LAUGHING WOMAN,
Diné (Navajo)

I do not understand this preoccupation of American historians with the earliest centuries of Indian/white contact, the colonial period, and the earliest decades of American nationhood; truly I do not understand it, for the very people who concern themselves with early origins and the founding of the republic are the ones most reluctant to talk to tribal elders who also deal with the origins, the beginning of the beginning of all beginnings. . . . The more I read history, the more I am convinced that history is modern man's mythology. Even the best of Western historical writing has no more meaning and no more truth value than what we have heretofore been pleased to term, with no little air of condescension, Indian mythology. . . .

The real directional thrust, the real vitality and tenacity of Indian cultures, derives from the traditional people, where they survive and are heeded. This is reason enough to have such an individual included in discussions of Indian history . . .

ALFONSO ORTIZ,
San Juan Pueblo

Crumbo

To us the ashes of our ancestors are sacred and
their resting place is hallowed ground. . . .
Every part of this soil is sacred in the
estimation of my people.

CHIEF SEATTLE,
Suquamish/Duwamish

I seek a direction from our elders, a trail to be
used by all Indians and based upon our
ancestry. . . . I believe strongly that [the]
Indian Spirit will be the last hope of mankind.
. . . Make it breathe by walking in the old
ways.

LORRENA DEAL,
Diné (Navajo)

You should understand
the way it was
back then,
because it is the same
even now.

LESLIE MARMON SILKO,
Laguna

Voices of Pride

I, Sarah Winnemucca, am a shell-flower, such as I wear on my dress. My name is Thocmetony. I am so beautiful! Who will come and dance with me while I am so beautiful? Oh, come and be happy with me! I shall be beautiful while the earth lasts.

SARAH WINNEMUCCA,
Paiute

Growing up poor has given me a sense of loyalty to working people, to the oppressed, and to the struggle for human dignity which I don't think I'll ever lose.

JACK D. FORBES,
Delaware-Powhatan-Saponi

Drafting of the Indians into the army is another wrong perpetrated upon the Indian without FIRST bestowing his just title—THE FIRST AMERICAN CITIZEN. Why not? He was here before Columbus, he was here before Washington, he was here before Lincoln and he was here and you came.

CARLOS MONTEZUMA,
Yavapai

What is important is that we have a superior way of life. We Indians have a more human philosophy of life. We Indians will show this country how to act human. Someday this country will revise its constitution, its laws, in terms of human beings, instead of property. If Red Power is to be a power in this country it is because it is ideological. . . . What is the ultimate value of a man's life? That is the question.

VINE DELORIA, JR.,
Sioux

Do you know what it takes to be an Indian? Essence. Those old people survived even when the pressure was great because they had it. Children at the BIA school with their braids cut off and in uniforms and shoes, they survived if they had a grandfather with essence. It's your spirit, the inner life, that I'm talking about, and it's the difference between what is Indian and what is not. This revised constitution is a joke, saying you can be Indian by blood. It's not blood . . .

ANNABELLE EAGLE,
Ute

In my youth the white society tempted me
with the apple of civilization and progress and
I ate it to the core and now I know its
dividends. Its path leads in two directions; one
to wealth and power; the other to poverty and
squalor. So, now I walk with only the Shell of
the turtle, having been gutted, but retaining
the stability of mind and spirit of my ancestors.

LOUISE OLIVER,
Muskogee/Yudri

I realized who I was, where I came from, and
that I would return to my people.

REGIS PECOS,
Cochiti Pueblo

Many people have asked me what my name
means. For years as a child I thought that it
was a name that the Whiteman gave to my
forefathers. One day while my wife was
working on our family tree she located the
name SUMDUM: the booming sound of the
ice as it is breaking from the glacier. Many
have said that my voice does boom. Hopefully
my poetry will boom across the state so that
others will not have to learn the hard way.

SHERMAN SUMDUM,
Tlingit

We always remember our veterans and show them respect for what they did. Even now, when I see the flag, I think of the veterans like my husband and my son, John, who served in Vietnam.

I don't think veterans get the respect that they should. . . .

So we are very proud of our veterans and on the 4th of July we always think of them.

JESSIE MANUELITO,
Paiute

It is the way I feel about the reservation—the land, the people and the culture—that makes it my home. I am from the reservation.

LAURA TOHE,
Diné (Navajo)

The trail of life can be how you see it.
Sometimes flowing or sad.
Remember the little skunk who said,
I own the road now.

JENNIE SEMINOLE PARKER,
Cheyenne

Voices of Hope

Every individual has a determination, a desire, a burning desire deep in his heart, and I'm sure that if every person can search for that, and reach for that, they will be successful in whatever they decide to do.

PETERSON ZAH,
Diné (Navajo)

Although wrongs have been done me I live in hopes.

BLACK KETTLE,
Cheyenne

Somewhere the healing process must begin. We have our differences, but we have so much to celebrate together—our strength, our beauty, our aspirations for our children. Their children are ours, ours are theirs. You only have to look to see that the Hopi and the Navajo are the two most beautiful people in the world.

ABBOTT SEKAQUAPTEWA,
Hopi